The Quilted Multiverse

Jill Munro

Fair Acre Press

First published 22nd April 2016 by Fair Acre Press

Copyright © Jill Munro 2016

The right of Jill Munro to be identified as the author of this work has been asserted by her in accordance with the Copyright, Designs and Patents Act 1988.

All rights reserved. No part of this publication may be reproduced, stored in or introduced into a retrieval system, or transmitted, in any form, or by any means (electronic, mechanical, photocopying, recording or otherwise) without the prior written consent permission of the publisher. Any person who does any unauthorised act in relation to this publication may be liable to criminal prosecution and civil claims for damages.

a CIP catalogue record for this book is available from the British Library

Printed and bound in Great Britain by Badger Print, Shropshire, UK

This book is sold subject to the condition that it shall not, by way of trade or otherwise, be lent, re-sold, hired out, or otherwise circulated without the publisher's prior consent in any form of binding or cover other than that in which it is published and without a similar condition including this condition being imposed on the subsequent purchaser.

Visit www.fairacrepress.co.uk for more about our books, podcasts, music, t-shirts, projects, competitions, author events, and subscription to our e-newsletter.

ISBN 9781911048176

Acknowledgements

The Mix was shortlisted for the Canterbury Festival Poet of the Year 2015 and printed in the Canterbury Festival Anthology 2015.

Woolf Wrote in Purple Ink was Highly Commended in the Sussex Poets' Competition 2015.

Freeze-framed was Highly Commended in the Charles Causley International Poetry Competition 2015.

The Quilted Multiverse

won

the 2016 International Fair Acre Press Poetry Pamphlet Competition

judged by Jonathan Edwards, whose debut collection
'My Family and Other Superheroes' received
the 2014 Costa Poetry Award

Praise for Jill Munro's *Man From La Paz:*
(Green Bottle Press 2015)

Munro comments both comically and insightfully on the everyday whilst entwining us in the apparitional. There's nothing commonplace in the collection.
    Abegail Morley

Jill Munro's arresting first collection brims with imagination. Sometimes spiky, often tender, no matter what the subject her eye remains thrillingly sharp.
    John McCullough

Formally dexterous, often provocative and occasionally surreal, these poems are infused with an exuberant sensuality and sly, irreverent wit.
    Catherine Smith

I love its physical and sensual exuberance, and willingness to tackle the everyday aspects of life with humour and unflinching gaze. This is a highly original collection.
    Sue Sims

For David, Jack & Lewey

Contents

9   I Married an AFOL*
10   She Sells Seashells
11   Woolf Wrote in Purple Ink
12   The Quilted Multiverse of Gardens
13   The Red Scarf
14   Jump Start
15   Every Breath You Take
16   Tinder
17   Freeze-framed
18   Hooked
20   Musical Ear Syndrome
21   The Mix
22   Butterflies
24   Five Stars
25   Subbuteo Man
26   Checkout
27   The Worst Poetry Workshop in the World
28   Rose Grows Old
29   Missing
30   Heart-throb
31   Girl in a Bright Blue Dress
32   Linda's Bedroom
33   The Court Verbatim Shorthand Reporter
34   Down Hill Road

36   About Jill Munro

I Married an AFOL*
*Adult Fan of Lego

The Sydney Opera house in the living room was the final straw.
At first it was small-scale – a pirate ship or two, a digger,
a cowboy fort; a Sopwith Camel flew by, it was all quite easy then.

Fairground rides began to spin, a Parisian bistro popped up.
His launching of the Maersk liner started off my wobble –
an Eiffel Tower sprouted and Pisa's white-washed leaner grew.

Along came Tower Bridge, complete with working drawbridge
spanning London's River Thames, with an accompanying
black cab and double-decker bus, thrown in just for fun.

But that unmistakable shell roofline & waterfront forecourt
overtook the carpet in the lounge and, oh, the non-stop raving
about the hard-to-find dark tan and white slant angled bricks,

the 48x48 baseplate *available in briny blue for the very first time!*
somewhat forced my move to a more expansive refuge –
the uncluttered floor of the interlocking house next door.

She Sells Seashells

Ray visits the busty blonde
daily on the shore to buy
a bucket of wet-glazed whorls —
seashells like sugar-varnished
Chelsea buns — and drops loose
change into her till of half-a-clam.

He sniffs his haul to recall
ocean days of kelp and krill,
scudding spume, wave & spray.
He'll be back tomorrow,
but tonight will dream
of a parting kiss from briny
lips, a coat-hem's glimpse
of a flash from her shiny tail.

Woolf Wrote in Purple Ink

and I do too but did that before
I knew and I know it's kind of childish
but I do just like the colour, the way
it makes a signature look – bold,
glamourous & cursive, even when it isn't –
and did you know she had a book
printed all in purple for her friend Violet?
The strange thing is that she was born
on the same day as my man –
just eighty years before him –
that probably doesn't really matter
either, apart from both being Aquarian,
other than she also wrote
we should all be a womanly man
or a manly woman, so in a unisex
kind of way that works too – him
not being her, of course, like I'm not
and also that stream of consciousness
way she wrote was really natty
and sort of left its purple modernist
mark, even if she wasn't left-handed
like me, though Nicole Kidman is
and had to learn to write right
handed for *The Hours* before loading
her pockets with stones, oozing
into that river to become a different
kind of water-carrier but another thing
she wrote is that for centuries
or so those who signed themselves
as *Anonymous* were, in all likelihood,
women which is probably the reason
she signed *Virginia Woolf* in purple ink.

The Quilted Multiverse of Gardens

When the train stalls to a slow graunch
along the track, the patchwork quilt
of urban Edens comes into view,
sewn and framed in creosote, barbed
wire, laurel bush or red stock bricks.

I spot the garden trimmed orange
in Sainsbury's bags stuffed
with papier-mâché magazines.
Next door the whirly-gig whizzes
on airy rounds, fixing smells of last night's

still smoking bonfire into hardening towels.
And there's the holey tennis net
looping low, once taut and high,
abandoned rackets on the lawn –
the kids gone in for tea or good.

And then it comes – a glimpse of backyard
heaven – a huge brilliant blue trampoline
stretching to square boundaries, where
a floral-aproned grandma is bouncing high,
higher, dreaming of another universe.

The Red Scarf

You said
we should
come back
every year
on this date
to this spot
to our Pine
where we sat
drank hot tea
ate brownies
that I'd made
carved hearts
into its bark
crushed fungi
with our backs
kissed and kissed
until our lips
were dry as leaves
You said
we should loop
our scarves
onto this branch
just like now
so we'd feel
like this
each year
at this spot
my scarf
bright green
yours was red
I did as
You said
every year
I did as
You said

Jump Start

He started small.
The playground's white lines, joins in the paving,
imaginary fissures in his mum's parquet.

Step on the crack and break your mother's back.

Who's to say what started it —
a fear of the devil lurking in the cracks,
old wives' folklore and frightening fable?

He even jumped the split in the middle
of the table, leap-frogging from rock salt
to black pepper then ketchupping back.

This boy was never found minding the gap.
He moved onto higher things — the Rocks
on the Common, pirouetting from stone to

mossy stone, especially when bored or alone.
Where is he now — our brave base-jumper?
Navigating space between sky-rise scrapers —

Step on the crack and break your mother's back

playing heart-stopping hopscotch on high Welsh hills.

Every Breath You Take

Back then when you were Blu-tacked
to my bedroom wall, I'd stand so
close to talk to you, wood-chip trapped
in your bee-striped top, punky gold locks aglow –
I'd sigh *The bed's too big without you…*

You sent your message – not in a bottle –
in a soft, teacherly Geordie brogue.
You warbled *Roxanne* just for me (*Outlandos D'Amour*
followed in the furry footsteps of *Wombling Free*).

Nightly you'd save me from walking the streets
for money, pull up at that wet bus stop, rhyme 'cough'
with 'Nabokov', halt my strut in sheer black ten-denier
thigh to toe, on patent high-heeled fives, transport me

to walk in *Fields of Gold*, fall into your arms, as my hair
came down whilst the west winds moved, as lovers do.
I longed to conjoin with you, yogi-like, linger in a ten-hour
bout of tantric sex, an endless jam session of joss-

sticky love but I was lost in my own jealous sky –
you married. Now I'm a Mrs, there's a final sting in the tail.
My man stands against the bedroom wall, gold hair
curls above his hum-coloured jumper. His words
I'll be watching you hang in the air.

Tinder

(after Shakespeare's Sonnet 129)

This application sees no waste in shame
Just lust, active lust, right swiped lust,
From the vacant, dull, hooded, blame
The savagely cruel youth, without trust
Who enjoys you soon, is not straight
Swiftly hunted, and so quickly had,
Promptly hated as a misused mate
You're cheaply laid by some callow lad
Bad in pursuit, too fast to come and go
Had, having, the screen's quest extreme;
No bliss in bed, or out, simply pained woe
A dream of urgent joy no less, still a dream.
    All this a girl well knows, does not know well
    To shun the sparking Tinderbox that leads to hell.

Freeze-framed

She keeps an invisible photo of him silver-framed on the side.
He's there – between the babies, brides and grads, jostling for space

amongst Cornish urchins, a Spanish flagon, that cracked
vase from Rhyl, the lighthouse striped in multi-coloured sand.

Sometimes she gives him a good dusting – unfolds his image
from the album in her skull, sees him through a time-lapse lens

and suddenly he's there – back to that one hot day – the rumpled
tartan rug, cold chicken, warm wine, his dark hair haloed

by periwinkle Padstow skies – soft voices, the sweet and salty
touch of a lover's lips, the cool, grey stare of a liar's eyes.

Hooked

It's not a crook I use
to hook the perfect man —
the cold, curved steel
knife held in my hand
flicks a slip-knot
draws back and forth
to make a chain, stitched
long and dangling free —
this could continue
indefinitely in its
linking, curling mail.

I turn and hook it
to a circle, complete
the round — to double
back or treble, Afghan
or a half, cluster
or a popcorn — choices
to be made in the witchery
of turning a single, thin
spun yarn to whatever
purpose I may choose:
squared shawl for a granny
soft cover for a baby
beanie for a boy-next-door
hand-made cushion for a craft stall
rough-hewn blanket for a refugee
holey bedspread for a tramp.

Instead, I hook my man —
a firm double crochet to form him —
steady, rugged, letting in no lacy airs,
warm flesh-coloured wool creates him
and *however you may imagine this*
is my chosen hue and no pattern
will be needed or left behind for any
hookers to follow in our wake.

Musical Ear Syndrome

I think she may be a little touched in the head, my mother.
She swears there's a wireless that keeps playing in her loft —

O Sole Mio! on a loop. She's had them all laddering up to check;
her neighbours, the *Elderly SOS* alarm man, the fire brigade —

and, of course, there's nothing to be found. She's worried
the radio may catch fire, short a fuse with never-ending

output, that the small Italian inside her head will prove incendiary.
He's only started singing like this since my father died last year.

I've told her to just enjoy the tune, let him serenade away
about his sun upon her face, the serenity after the storm,

the clear day with air so fresh it's like a celebration in her loft.
She says she thinks I may be a little touched in the head.

The Mix

We're pinnied. An earthenware bowl
rests on the old oak table, its inner white
glaze gluey with creamed Blue Band
and the rough grit graze of Tate & Lyle.
A split wooden spoon is buried
in the mix — beaten to Billericay
by my enamelled, Max-Factored mother
to prevent the eggy curdle.

A drip-drip of vanilla essence, before
Homepride Fred's hat dredging spoils
her spotless cloth. A spatula scrape,
spoon licked to immaculacy,
hot tinned Victoria sponge rise,
smell of rack-cooling, Robertson's
raspberry jam piled high,
sharp seeds suspended.

No, Asantewa can't come to tea
ask Anne, Kathy, Susie…

I cut the paper golly free
from his label, release him
to the neat worktop stack
of an elastic band of brothers
to be sent for the amazing
golly-morph to enamel lapel badge;
the collectable golly-golfers, cricketers,
jugglers, ice-skaters and fishermen
who multiplied slave-like on my cardi —
a smiling gang of golly friends
now safely pinned in time.

Butterflies

I will not pull the wings off butterflies
like the smallness of feathers or leaves

or purple emperors, painted ladies or
I am about yearning and I have turned

I vaguely remember called Ria who could
between tablecloths on the breakfast

screamed and I find myself sitting on a park
like Cheltenham or Eastbourne next to a

knowing there's more to life than being a
knowing there's something out there to

can or can't be caught but if held too tight-

or feel their soft brush against my thighs
alighting for nano-seconds in a rush of red

silver-washed fritillaries on the day I discover
slowly but steadily into a sit-com character

n't cook and piled the dishes in layer after layer
table and no-one wondered why she silently

bench somewhere that could be anywhere
man who might or might not be named Leonard

lepidopterist or a mother or a wife or a poet
be lunged for that may or may not be reached

ly might just get squashed   all over your hand.

Five Stars

Nothing's too much trouble for our stellar host –
he bellows loud hellos from his front door
before our car-bound feet disrupt his gravel.

Call-me-Toby ushers us to his spongey lemon couch
for a slice of just-baked drizzling lemon sponge cake.
He plunges into freshly brewed fairly-traded coffee,

pours into bone-china, places saucers on *Badger's Bottom
B&B* logoed coasters – smooth moving in Oxford-blue chinos.
Beaming, he returns enthused from a baggage carry

past the rows of rosettes and constellations in his hall,
to point out the silver optics of his honesty bar, pen poised.
He plumps bum-dented tasseled tapestry, clears crockery,

as the whites of his teeth promise dawn's Aga-griddled
home-bred hens' eggs, free-range sausages, bacon too,
herb-tossed mushrooms, grilled English toms (never tinned).

Garden-hived honey biscuits crumble by a gleaming kettle,
wrapped dark chocs settle on puffed-up Egyptian duck down
pillows; a call from below 'If off early, do let me de-ice you.'

A cool karma pervades the tile-hot his 'n' hers en-suite –
tea-tree infused wipes, handmade peach soaps *by AnnMarie*,
whilst nostril-numbing citrus wick drifts like a charm.

Next morning, rainfall shower-drenched, steam-blind, I reach
for the fluff of white warmed by the ladder-rack – and there he is,
towel held wide as Cassiopeia, ready to enwrap his guest.

Subbuteo Man

rock on your own
hemisphere kick spin

save score dive here
die-hard loyal fan man

let me sniff the musk
of your cool plastic

hear silence in colours
of constant support

model team player tie
a scarf around your mouth

suppress all sounds of love
the fuzzy gag that's

clawed us close wed
hands here on soft green

baize while white lines
contain the smell of turf sweat

goals whistle through us
our match binds and keeps us

from the subsuming crowd
Man you're mine

Checkout

This green-striped girl who works the till
is topped with a sunburst smile, her wrists
tattooed with bracelets of Greek keys.
She speaks of the future. Her barcodes
tell of what will be – if the blueberries
won't scan today, Chelsea will win away and if
the strawberries are on three for two, it's bound
to be another Grand Slam win for Murray.
She scans pre-packed Icebergs, tells me to listen
to their urgent beeps, not with my ears
but with my lettuce heart, to feel the pulse
of what her reader's saying.

I listen to the Morse code of salad stuff –
the di-dah-di-dit as she passes prediction
to the neon red flashes of Cos and Radicchio,
where Romaines and radishes are kings.
Chicory at rest in trays of polystyrene
waits for her fortune-telling hands of nail-bright
Cherry Red to fling them further on their passage
from far off lorry routes of Lincolnshire
on their final trip to fridge drawer heaven.

She grins like Demeter, a Greek goddess with
deep plum-tinted hair, to the trill of Kenyan
purple-sprouting broccoli and packeted
Peruvian asparagus – *ooo, I'd love to go there
for my hols, take all my saved up airmiles to Peru* –
and together we can hear the easy-peeler
tangerines hold their collective breath,
before they scream of foreign shores.

The Worst Poetry Workshop in the World

begins with the arrival of my dead father
who states his views on poetry:
*Can't see the point of it — it's just like
listening to other people's dreams*
before realising he's appearing in one.
Paper and pens and prompts and time
start to run out and up he pipes again
*Take that girl with her Tesco poem — she
should get to the point before the checkout.*

The plate of biscuits prompt fails abysmally
until I see the boy with dead-fly eyes,
a digestive heart, party rings for ears.
I pass over the chocolate hob-nobs.

We all read our efforts and it's then I find
he's right — I should get to the point
before the checkout.

Rose Grows Old

She runs a faded floral walking stick
along the playground railings of St Richard's,
pied pipers children near with her ritual
ratchet-clack of wood on iron.
She mutters *There's no money for butter*
as she reaches into caverns in her seams,
takes out sweet handfuls in shiny wrappers
to pass through gaps to palms
that fist-scrunch tight their bounty
before the clanger call to class.

Rose slumps down to take a tired
pavement seat – she's a string-belted damson
ready for the jamming. With pale summer
gloved hands she reaches for each slipper,
squeezes out showers from lilac fluff,
plucks a leaky marker pen from a store
in her red fedora's hatband, begins
scribing with her left hand on her wrinkled
right, puckered with tattooed
symbols no-one can understand.

From an inner pocket in her wool, she pulls
a tarnished hipflask, brandy warms her gullet,
catches fingers in amethyst dreads of hair,
spits smiles and swear words at passers-by,
gobbles on a furred, black sausage,
mumbles *When I am old, when I am old…*

Missing

I pin your poster high up on a tree –
a plastic cover saves you from the rain.
I want each grown-up passer-by to see
your olive almond eyes, the collar chain

that bears your tiny name, enwraps your neck,
the glint of off-white so soft satin hair.
I want them all to feel my need, to check
their sheds. I want you back with me, sat there –

chair-curled, round and fur-balled on my lap,
not ink-run, paper-fading on a post.
I want to hear the thud of the cat-flap,
the quiet purring Missy I love most.

But it's my fate to wait alone and cry
for you – the one my parents wouldn't buy.

Heart-throb

I look into bright anti-freeze blue
eyes with instant recognition for a man

I always knew would be waiting for me
but not necessarily behind this door.

I take my seat, still lost in lashes.
Dilated pupils stare into naked skulls.

You move closer to roll my cashmere sleeve –
you'd be fanning feathers if you had them –

Velcro me to you, connect by a wire,
a tube, ramp up the air between us.

You attune your switches, a twitch of metal
intrudes, an unwelcome whiff of rubber drifts

on warmth. The squeeze, the vice-like
grip of a tubeless tyre, the rock of your head,

a barely-there smile, a grind of teeth on teeth,
the press of pink flesh on flesh, the deflation.

Please do it again, just once more, in case.
It's sudden – this all-consuming crush –

as red digits flash-dance before us.
You sigh, declare a dose-doubling necessary.

It's the effect I have, Dr Peacock says,
maybe white-coat syndrome but all

*my female patients of middling years, though not ill,
are on 4 milligrams per day of Perindopril.*

Girl in a Bright Blue Dress

This girl is initialled in an A-line of Disney blue,
reflects banana blonde into a crack of glass
bottles herself in childhood fractals
of cats and queens, hookahs and hats.

This girl lives to question the golden trip,
croquets her footsteps when large turns little
with one poisonous slurp, flavoured cherry
tart, roast turkey, custard buttered toast.

This girl transforms – goes in search
of where she's been or going, failing,
eats, doesn't eat, imbibes, pukes pink
as a flamingo on a road to lose her head.

The caterpillar smokes on, exhales his riddles –
all mushroom memories turn butterfly.

Linda's Bedroom
i.m. Linda Cameron, 1954-1986

Pulmonary Emboli, in case you're wondering.

I'm ten, you're seventeen. The citrus stench
of Aqua Manda mixes with Rive Gauche.
Walls of stylised orange-eyed daisies climb through
vines, the slope of the Velux lets in air to clear
the cling. Your floor is strewn with Simplicity patterns

for minis and hot-pants; velvet, crimping shears,
hooks & eyes. Boot-laces lick at a Flokati rug, –
your Astrakhan Orinoco coat Wombles free.
Jim Morrison cool-eyes from an album cover,
fine art Rotring nibs leak, blot sketch pads.

Water-colours of my own green-eyed, smiling face
scramble on your desk. I rifle through pine drawers
to nick a new decimal ten pence for Palma Violets.
A little sister's curiosity cannot resist your furry diary,
reads *I think I'm in love with Brian Allen…*

Photo-me fours of you laughing with a blue-eyed
boy fall from scribbled pages. I spot a secret –
the day-marked silver foil of The Pill –
and all the bedroom's eyes widen.

The Court Verbatim Shorthand Reporter

I have wielded my pencil like a sword at 140 words per minute
to record the minor mis-doings of the inhabitants of Staines,
frantically squiggled dots, dashes, chays, jays, hays and yays –

in days before a 'hay' or a 'yay' was a common greeting
and Pitman 2000 sounded so futuristic
at around a double-decade ahead of its dating.

I have taken down all the evidence for Mister Harold Seed,
Clerk to the Justices, Dickensian in name and deed.
I have demolished notepad after notepad, beaten to death

my old manual Adler's qwerty keys, carriage-returned
with a relentless 'ding', discretely cursed every error
and the ritual rubbing through four purple carboned

layers that often resulted in a hole. I have been slim,
pencil-skirted, unruffled by defendants' misdemeanors;
the gangrenous flasher with his vital appendage

about to drop, stinking out the courtroom, even
though shielded by flapping greasy gabardine.
The day came when I lost this teenage pencil-poise,

my modish rhubarb-coloured legs wobbled as the Warrant
Officer announced the next defendant, a milkman
charged with discrepancies in the billing of his round,

dodgy dealings at the dairy – a Mr. Bernard Malcolm Lawson.
Suspicions were confirmed on peering from my pad –
there stood my Uncle Malc, milk-white on the stand.

Down Hill Road

Eileen wears a coat of sunshine
having shed her winter pelt
of worn teddy-brown astrakhan
which warmed her against
nearly-no degrees of Celsius

and the dull belted trench which layered
her from February's splash
and drizzle, nearly covered the cloth
of her fraying knees. They peeped –
two puffed white boulders –

from the edge of her beige buckled hem.
Now March is out and nearly April too –
she's cast her clout and makes her way
along Hill Road to Lidl for chops and gin.
She wonders if she may have gone a bit

too far with her early casting
in the new spring season's
coat of simple, straight-lined rays,
wheeling her plaid shopping trolley
chilled, stark naked, down Hill Road.

About Jill Munro

In 2015, Jill had two poems long-listed for the National Poetry competition, was shortlisted for Canterbury Poet of the Year, highly commended in the Sussex Poets' Competition & the Princemere Poetry Prize and had her first collection, *Man from La Paz*, published by *Green Bottle Press*, London.

In 2016, she has been short-listed for the Charles Causley International Poetry Prize and is the winner of the inaugural Fair Acre Press Pamphlet Competition.

She agrees with the late Charles Causley, that without writing poetry she would 'explode'.

Man from La Paz is available from www.greenbottlepress.com.